# We live among strangers

Savannah, Georgia

Selected Poems

By

Willie Dean, Jr

# Dedication

For them that made the ultimate sacrifice in the struggle for Black Liberation

# Acknowledgement

Thank you to all those brothers and sisters, warriors, and freedom fighters, prophetic voices, who spoke truth to power, in the face of brutality, racism, and murder, your sacrifice has not been in vain.
Ase', Hotep.

# Table of Contents

# Introduction

## Chapbook of the Black Experience

This Chapbook of selected poems deals with the black experience in America. A glimpse into the lives of black people, who endured 400 years of degradation and humiliation, a salute to all the freedom fighters of black liberation. It's a mosaic of pain, suffering, love, laughter, and triumph.

# Daydreaming

Looking out /the windows/we called/it the field-

its baring/now/lost to another time/cheers/people/the gathering.

The crack of the bat/sun drenched/skies/

turning to dusk/at sunset/streetlights beaming/wooden poles

mama's voices/ echoes off the pavement/

Pete's corner store/baseball/memories

of my loss loved one.

# The Broken Two

If you see me walking down the street/you unhesitatingly cross/if I speak up you label me/aggressive/when I'm silent// somehow I appear weak/broken spirited/my woman thinks me aloof/society thinks me/a menace/ my silence protects// my fierceness deflects/daddy left/he too angry and depressed//now imprisoned for life//since his youth he had to fight/why are you surprised//when I say, I don't cry//when you turn away your eyes// when you corrupted/ my history with your lies//black male suicide on the rise//because his image despised/if you really knew//inside//there's two//desperate to be free.

## *Courage*

*Often I pretend, not to hear, the anguish and despair/of distant lands afar/even when listening to NPR//I pretend/recently I read of John Quincy Adams// anti-slavery//founding fathers under the yoke of tyranny//decisions, decisions//many of whom themselves slave holders//picked up arms/JFK wrote of profiles in Courage// later slain by the assassins bullet/A Nation founded in blood and rebellion//but not for the melanated ones//A flawed Constitution//refused restitution//three-fifths clause//manipulated for their selfish cause//lately I pretend//but the sin//permeates my skin//self-muzzled//guilt and shame//legacy, I must reclaim//my ancestors defamed//a true picture of profiles in Courage//I get it, I get it; exclaimed//therefore we speak//out of Courage.*

# Penny Hustle

Back in the day, I guess around 9 or 10, we would gather in the alley, the bare wall facing us, with graffiti written all over it. Maybe five or six guys, laughing and giggling and pitching pennies, some days you win and other days you lose. But mama didn't know, my daddy, he was a gambler too, so he wouldn't care. They played the street numbers too. Dreaming someday of getting rich, but not today because all we had going at the time was the penny hustle.

## *For want of Love*

*Often you have heard it said that the eyes are the gateway to the soul...it's like*

*standing on your tiptoes peering through a keyhole. I'm reminded of my parents admonition.*

*always look the person in the eye, while most would look away...*

*for fear of what the eyes will say.*

*Fear and trembling...*

*abound, have you considered, the idea*

*of the computer was the result of studying the heart.*

*With its deep storage space, the heart holds all the stories of one's life.*

*Greed, Lust, Envy, Gluttony, Sloth, Pride, Wrath...*

*You know them, the 7 Deadly Sins.*

*Man's time on earth is but a blur, yet he spends it in*

*struggles.*

*Why, you might ask, next time you bump into*

*him/her*

*peek into the eye...then wait on it...*

*if you listen intently, it will*

*reply,*

*For want of love!*

## *We live among strangers*

*Like a broken branch plucked from the mother tree, floats to the ground-
never to regain that place of harmony, trampled upon, covered
beneath the other brother and sister leaves, who too have been
displaced, like the scars of a battered woman's face, or the young
man trying to find his place- looked upon, and disgraced, passed
over, stepped on, stepped on...not long-ago force to ride in the back
of the bus. The Great Migration a plan of relief, from beneath the
policeman's jack boot, wedged into the ghettos of northern despair,
crowded tenements, poverty hovering like a dirty cloud of polluted
air. I never asked for a handout, but the opportunity to stand out, the
Central Park 5 proclaimed, if you don't see me? Stokely coined
black power, signaling, we have had enough, forces at play,
structural barriers, no social compact for them they say. The
crucifixion of my people, dare I say- no pity, stand in need of, to do
so is to absolve you for denying my humanity.*

# Detroit, 1967

It was one of the hottest summers days.

In July 1967, unknown to me as a child, this day

of all days would forever take away my childhood.

The tension in the Black community

was palpable.

The Christmas before, my brother

and I received our plastic toy M16 rifles.

It was gray and black plastic with the handle,

on top to carry. Like what I'd witness,

the soldiers carry on the nightly

news in

Vietnam.

It was the day the soldiers rolled down my block,

Four to a jeep, long guns in hand, carbines, and M16's.

Playing in the field across from my house.

The sound of my toy M16 roared.

Running,

ducking and dodging imaginary bullets flying…my brother and I played

on.

Suddenly, the tires screeched to a halt,

and the soldiers, in green

fatigues,

leaped from the jeep screaming and aiming,

their weapons at us.

Yelling out for my mama, mama, mama, mama,

as I dropped my toy M16,

darting by the troops, leaping across the street,

never noticing if my feet touch the surface,

stumbling as I tried to climb two steps,

at a time.

That was the day, the troops rolled down my block,

with their fingers on the trigger, and the hammer

unlock.

Like a virgin stripped of her virginity by force,

they snatched my childhood from me,

at the barrel of an M16.

## *Walk with our Ancestors*

*Clap boards, clap boards//shotgun shacks/shotgun shacks//*

*red clay mud//beneath their feet//*

*the only place//to rest our backs/*

*acres and acres//plantations roll//*

*white balls//foliage//strange fruit//*

*segregation/white and colored signs// Bull Connor/*

*Bombingham//4 little girls/Medgar shot// Bobby Hutton*

*and the Black Messiah//Black Liberation//*

*pouring out libations//we erect//*

*ancestor altars//striking a white candle//*

*In Memoriam*

## *Apology to the Black Woman*

*Just the other day, my wife shared with me a conversation,*
*she had with her Sister Circle, that she didn't want to be a hard*
*woman, that she wants to be a soft woman...*
*there, I was transported back to my childhood home,*
*a two-family flat.*
*Standing in the middle of my living room, in this grown man body,*
*seeing, and reliving the mental and physical abuse, endured.*
*Like many women of her generation who suffered in silence,*
*at the hands of abusive black men.*
*Wondering if they ever had a moment of happiness.*
*Generation, after generation of broken hearts, and*
*emptiness.*
*Bodies not their own, raped, beaten, cheated on.*
*Finally, abandoned and left alone. Forced to stay,*
*and raise children, and build a home...*
*black men its time we right this wrong. Today,*
*mama, I say, I'm sorry, to my sisters, I'm sorry, to my wife,*
*I'm sorry, to my niece, I'm sorry, to the queen's of the*
*Universe, I'm sorry, no more tears to shed,*
*niggas, know we were misled.*
*Stand up black man, and apologize to the black woman,*
*if she's hard, its because we were soft.*
*I apologize, I apologize, I apologize to the black woman.*
*Ase'*

# *Haiku*

## *Sophisticated Negro*

*Sophisticated negro,*

*black beaver bowler, gray tweed suit,*

*with brown spats.*

# *Haiku*

## Black Revolutionary

to be a revolutionary,

 one must open, one's mouth,

then struggle on, struggle on.

# *Haiku*

## The System

The system,

rap with brother, Wile E. Coyote,

even he knows the game is rigged.

## Growing up, Detroit

I always knew. I had to go, had to go, the tug,
of the spirit deep…growing up on
17<sup>th</sup> street. The turbulent years of the sixties.
The Bishops and The Chains, well know street gangs.
On my block the Black Panther Party, I remember,
the leaflets on storefronts, with the black
panther logo emblazoned, this was a
time of mimeograph machines.
What in my immature state, would draw
me into this scene? Ignorant to the dangers surrounding the party,
Slowly, slowly, an invisible force had laid hold of me.
It was the birth of the Motown sound, with doo rags, processed hair,
shark skinned pants, bandlon knit shirts, and Beatles shoes.
Marvin Gaye asked, "What's going on"?
It was my coming of age, pimps, players, and prostitutes.
Black power salutes, afros, and right on slogans too.
Detroit, once known as the murder capital.
To outsiders, with its violence, could be a scary place.
I even noticed on TV shows,
we were always depicted in police dramas,
or action flicks, with pejorative story lines…
drugs, poverty, gangsters, all things
stereotyped.

Despite all, Detroit, was a thriving and prosperous city,

Historians even labeled Detroit the Paris of America.

Those days are behind us now, and for me, although,

I left 25 years ago. With melancholic memories, it will always be home.

### When we all grow up

*If you've ever driven on I-20 in Atlanta, in the mornings,*
*you know that it can be a nightmare,*
*bumper to bumper traffic, on this brisk day,*
*as I head into my office,*
*post covid, working a hybrid schedule, which is fine by me.*
*Although if I had my way,*
*I would just work from home.*
*As I sat in traffic, with the radio turn to NPR,*
*in the background,*
*depending on my mood sometimes,*
*it will be on WCLK, the jazz station.*
*To my right there is construction going on, as I glanced up,*
*the amber glow of the tree tips came into view.*
*I used to drink coffee, but now just herbal tea, but*
*I didn't have a cup in the car this morning.*
*A drive that would normally take thirty minutes, during*
*normal days, will take me forty-five minutes, sometimes,*
*an hour.*
*But the drive allows me to hear the stories of real people,*
*dealing with real issues, in a real world from*
*across the American landscape and of course*
*internationally.*
*Somedays, I will ride in silence, loss in my on*

*thoughts and imagination.*

*On this day, as I listen to the stories shared on NPR,*

*the thought occurred to me, in the form of a question.*

*What do people really want? Most of us want more money,*

*more time with family and friends, more freedom, and yes more sex,*

*yeah, more sex, if you don't*

*then you don't know what you're missing.*

*But I digress, in a world beset, with all sorts of problems,*

*from poverty, sadness, hopelessness, war, homelessness,*

*and despair.*

*My wife and I often say that everyone has a story,*

*imagine, if we took the time, to listen to each other's,*

*stories, what kind of world it could be.*

*As my mind came out of its state of solitude, and meditation,*

*and I was brought back to my drive along I-20.*

*In that instant, a second question came to me,*

*What kind of people we could be?*

*When we all grow up.*

## Sonnet
### Will to be

*If there's no place for me to call home, tis better that I be left alone,*
*If there's no role in your society, tis better if one step aside an avoid acrimony,*
*If there's nothing to look forward to than the vicissitudes of life,*
*If there's only, hatred, bigotry, and strife, give each a knife,*
*If there's only the rich and the poor, how then to even the score,*
*If there's only nationalism, populism, and favoritism,*
*If there's only violence, bloodshed, and war...*

*Will to be, better than our ancestors, before,*
*Will to be, generous, kind and loving at your core,*
*Will to be, friendly, honest, trustworthy, the more,*
*Will to be, compassionate, empathetic, and brave,*
*Will to be, different, than a brainwashed knave,*
*Will to be, happy, and not afraid,*
*Will to be, a human being, just a human being.*

## *No Wasted Tears*

In hopes of arousing us all from the
slumber of our collective lethargy.
On a very hot and humid night in the delta,
of Mississippi.
Fireflies gave off light as they buzzed about,
Immersed in the woods of the grand white oaks, sat a one room,
shack, surrounded by swamps, the frogs croaked, a sad melody.
It was the rise of the night riders, angry hooded whites, who bleed and
and died during the Civil War.
Determined to preserve their way of life, on the backs,
of free labor, a system of deprivation, humiliation,
wrought, by economic exploitation, subjugation,
with the blessing of the U.S. Administration.
Off in the distance the night riders, whispered,
we will teach them niggers, a lesson, a lesson,
the world will not soon forget. It was, the beginning,
of terrorism, one hundred years of lynching.
It was the echoing refrain; this is a white man's city.
From the moonlight, the sweat beaded up on the horse's mane,
so much so that the horses appeared to be angry,
their nostrils flared, they kicked up their front legs, as if under the
influence of some psychedelic.
By dawn, as the sun rose, the shack smoldered from the flames.

There, in the front yard, dangled the mangled bodies of the,

man, woman, and child, from the grand white oak,

their crime, being black in the delta of Mississippi.

In the 21$^{st}$ century, in Florida, New York, Ohio, Ferguson, Louisville,

and Minnesota, Day riders roam the city streets, off in the distance,

uniformed whites in cruisers, whispered, let's take back our country, division,

fuel by hatred, and bigotry.

As we wipe away the rheum, and shake of the lethargy,

in our collective imaginations, let us remember,

the warriors, the freedom fighters, the innocent, as we

carved their names in the book of

No Wasted Tears.

# Images of the Black Experience

**ALSO, BY WILLIE DEAN, JR**

Eventide Poems

Blackbird Collection of Poems

Email Address

Wjdean769@gmail.com

*"We were aware of the fact that death walks hand in hand with struggle".*

*Stokely Carmichael*

www.ingramcontent.com/pod-product-compliance
Lightning Source LLC
Chambersburg PA
CBHW030529130626
46549CB00007B/3159